Navy SEALs

by Julie Murray

ABDO
U.S. ARMED FORCES
Kids

www.abdopublishing.com

Published by Abdo Kids, a division of ABDO, PO Box 398166, Minneapolis, Minnesota 55439.

Printed in the United States of America, North Mankato, Minnesota.

052014

092014

 THIS BOOK CONTAINS
RECYCLED MATERIALS

Photo Credits: AP Images, Getty Images, Shutterstock, Thinkstock, © U.S. Navy p.1, © Official
U.S. Navy Imagery / CC-BY-2.0 p. 5, 11, © Journalist 3rd Class Davis J. Anderson p.9, © DVIDSHUB /
CC-BY-2.0 p.13, © Senior Chief Mass Communication Specialist Andrew McKaskle p.21

Production Contributors: Teddy Borth, Jennie Forsberg, Grace Hansen

Design Contributors: Candice Keimig, Laura Rask, Dorothy Toth

Library of Congress Control Number: 2013953953

Cataloging-in-Publication Data

Murray, Julie.
 Navy SEALs / Julie Murray.
   p. cm. -- (U.S. Armed Forces)
 ISBN 978-1-62970-092-2 (lib. bdg.)   6612224
 Includes bibliographical references and index.

1. United States Navy SEALS--Juvenile literature. 2. United States Navy--Commando troops--
Juvenile literature. 3. Special operations (Military science)--Juvenile literature. 4. Special Forces
(Military science)--Juvenile literature. I. Title.

359.9--dc23

                2013953953

Table of Contents

Navy SEALs

Navy SEALs are a special group in the **military**. They are part of the U.S. Navy.

5

Navy SEALs carry out secret jobs around the world. They are ready for any **situation**.

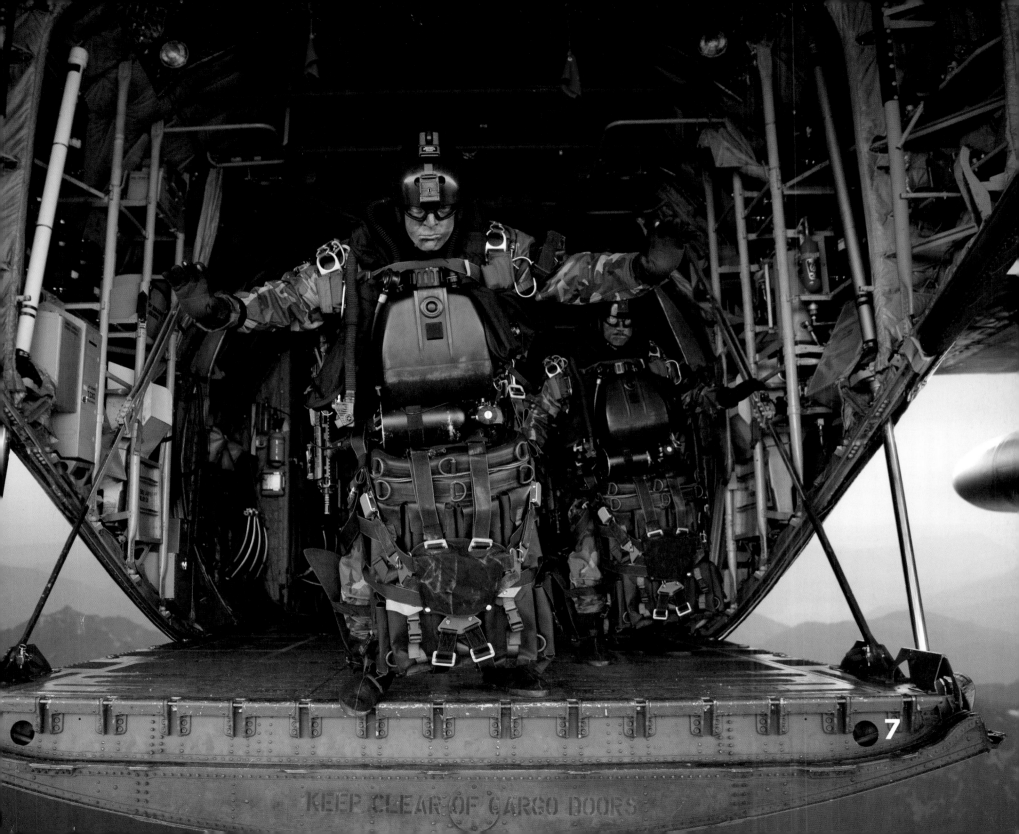

KEEP CLEAR OF CARGO DOORS

7

Navy SEALs stands

for **SE**a, **A**ir, and **L**and.

8

Only men can be Navy SEALs. They have to have good eyesight. They also have to be 28 years old or younger.

Training to be a Navy SEAL is very hard. It lasts for 30 months.

Jobs

Navy SEALs gather information about the enemy. They also attack enemy targets.

Many Navy SEALs' jobs are done at night. They use night-vision goggles. These help them see in the dark.

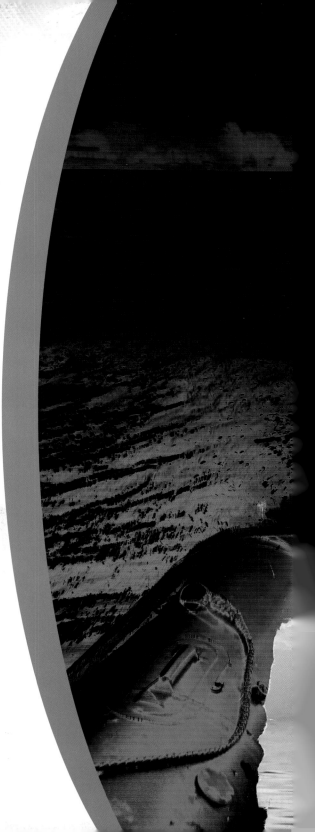

Weapons and Machines

Navy SEALs use rubber boats called **Zodiacs**. They also use parachutes and guns.

"The Only Easy Day Was Yesterday"

Navy SEALs keep

Americans safe every day!

More Facts

- Navy SEALs are trained especially for combat in surprise **strikes**.

- Navy SEALs have very specialized training for sea, land, and air missions.

- The Navy SEALs make up about 1% of the United States Navy **personnel**.

Glossary

military – the armed forces of a nation.

personnel – people employed by an organization, business, or service.

situation – an event or problem that one finds oneself in.

strike – a sudden attack, usually a military one.

zodiac – heavy duty, inflatable boats used for missions.

Index

abdokids.com

Use this code to log on to abdokids.com and access crafts, games, videos and more!

Abdo Kids Code:
UNK0922